FLY

THROUGH
THE BIBLE

A BRIEF INTRODUCTION

COLIN S. SMITH

MOODY PUBLISHERS

CHICAGO

Portions of this book were previously published as sermons on openthebible.org. Used by permission.

All Scripture quotations, unless otherwise indicated, are from the ESV® Bible (The Holy Bible, English
Standard Version®), © 2001 by Crossway, a publishing ministry of Good News Publishers. Used by permission.
All rights reserved. The ESV text may not be quoted in any publication made available to the public by a
Creative Commons license. The ESV may not be translated in whole or in part into any other language.

Scripture quotations marked (NIV) are taken from the Holy Bible, New International Version®, NIV®.
Copyright © 1973, 1978, 1984, 2011 by Biblica, Inc.™ Used by permission of Zondervan. All rights
reserved worldwide. www.zondervan.com The "NIV" and "New International Version" are trademarks
registered in the United States Patent and Trademark Office by Biblica, Inc.™

Edited by Kevin Mungons
Interior design: Puckett Smartt
Cover design: Brittany Schrock
Cover background wavy stripes copyright © 2023 by jackreznor/Adobe Stock (625642836). All rights reserved.
Cover photo of forest by Fotis Fotopoulos, courtesy of Unsplash.

Library of Congress Cataloging-in-Publication Data

Names: Smith, Colin S., 1958- author.
Title: Fly through the Bible : a brief introduction / Colin S. Smith.
Description: Chicago : Moody Publishers, [2024] | Includes bibliographical
  references. | Summary: "The view from above is majestic! Smith helps you
  find the right altitude to take in the big-picture landscape of God's
  story. Even if you've never opened the Bible, this short flight will
  introduce you to God's Word and leave you marveling at how it all fits
  together"-- Provided by publisher.
Identifiers: LCCN 2023057954 (print) | LCCN 2023057955 (ebook) | ISBN
  9780802434548 (paperback) | ISBN 9780802470850 (ebook)
Subjects: LCSH: Bible--Introductions. | Bible--Study and teaching. | BISAC:
  RELIGION / Biblical Studies / General | RELIGION / Biblical Commentary /
  General
Classification: LCC BS475.3 .S649 2024 (print) | LCC BS475.3 (ebook) |
  DDC 220.6076--dc23/eng/20240213
LC record available at https://lccn.loc.gov/2023057954
LC ebook record available at https://lccn.loc.gov/2023057955

Originally delivered by fleets of horse-drawn wagons, the affordable paperbacks from D. L. Moody's
publishing house resourced the church and served everyday people. Now, after more than 125 years of
publishing and ministry, Moody Publishers' mission remains the same—even if our delivery systems have
changed a bit. For more information on other books (and resources) created from a biblical perspective, go
to www.moodypublishers.com or write to:

Moody Publishers
820 N. LaSalle Boulevard
Chicago, IL 60610

1 3 5 7 9 10 8 6 4 2

Printed in the United States of America

For Bev Savage
Godly Pastor
Wise Mentor
Dearly Loved Friend

CONTENTS

INTRODUCTION

SUPPOSE YOU ARE PLANNING a trip to the Grand Canyon. Your aim is to explore this vast wonder that is 277 miles long, up to eighteen miles wide, and over a mile deep. Where would you begin?

If you chose to drive close to the rim, you would get a sense of the canyon's length and width, but not its depth. If you chose to hike down the canyon, you would discover its depth and its width, but not its length.

Driving and hiking would enable you to experience the canyon in different ways, but if you had the opportunity to take a flight over the Grand Canyon, that would be the best way to begin.

A flight would also have its limitations. There is a world of wonders that you could only discover with your feet on the ground. But a flight over the canyon would show you its vastness and beauty and gaining that perspective would help you to know what to look for when you drive around the rim or hike down to the river.

Fly Through the Bible is a high-altitude exploration of the entire Bible story. With so much to cover we're going to move quickly. But I hope that this brief introduction to the Bible will help you grasp who God is, who you are, who Jesus is, and what He offers to you.

Our journey begins with the Old Testament, where we're going to meet five people: Adam, Abraham, Moses, David, and Ezra.

Then in the Gospels we will look at five events from the life of Jesus: His birth, temptations, crucifixion, resurrection, and ascension. Then in the New Testament letters we will consider five gifts of God to all who believe: The Holy Spirit, faith, forgiveness, the church, and heaven.

The Bible tells us stories from another time and place, so don't be surprised if some things seem strange or unfamiliar. Don't let that put you off. When you open the Bible, you will discover a whole new world.

Maybe you are thinking, *I'm not sure I believe the Bible.* That's okay. I'm glad you're taking the tour. Please listen to what God has said and look at what He has done. You may find that, far from being a relic of the past, the Bible is the means by which God speaks to you today.

PART 1

FIVE PEOPLE
IN THE
OLD
TESTAMENT

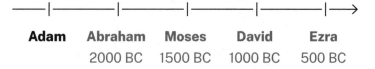

Adam   **Abraham**   **Moses**   **David**   **Ezra**

2000 BC   1500 BC   1000 BC   500 BC

Who am I? Why am I here? And why is the world as it is?
All of us ask these questions. Our lives are affected deeply
by the decisions and behavior of our parents. For better or worse,
who they were and what they did have a profound effect on us.
The Bible tells us that our first parents were created by God
for a great and glorious purpose. But the decisions they made
brought ruin and disaster that we still live with today.

1

ADAM

THE BIBLE BEGINS by telling us that God created the heavens and the earth (Genesis 1:1). God made the sun, the moon, and the stars. Then He made the plants, fish, birds, and animals. But God's masterpiece was still to come.

> Then God said, "Let us make man in our image, after our likeness." (Genesis 1:26)

The Hebrew word translated "man" here is *adam*. That's where the first man got his name. Adam was made in the image of God, and what was true of him is true of you. You are made in the image of God. An image is a reflection. God made you in such a way that you reflect something of His nature and glory. That means your life has unique dignity and worth.

God made Adam by forming a corpse from the dust of the ground. Then He breathed into it, and Adam became a living being

(Genesis 2:7). From this we learn, first, that our minds and bodies are fragile, and second, that our lives are a gift from God, and that we are always dependent on Him.

God filled Adam's life with wonderful gifts. He planted a garden and gave it to Adam as his home (Genesis 2:8). He gave Adam the fulfilling work of naming the animals and participated in Adam's work by bringing the animals to him (Genesis 2:19). But God saw that it was not good for Adam to be alone. He created Eve and then "brought her to the man," and she became his wife (Genesis 2:22).

Home, work, and marriage are good gifts from God. *Home* is where God sets you down. No home is perfect, but the best place to flourish is the place God has prepared for you.

Work is what God gives you to do. God's work brings order out of chaos; He creates what is beautiful; He protects and provides for all that He has made. And when you do these things in your work, you reflect the work of God.

Marriage is God's gift of union with another person. The first marriage had its share of troubles, but whatever their problems, Adam and Eve could never have doubted that they had been joined together by God.

But the greatest gift of God to Adam and Eve was the gift of His friendship. God is invisible, but He appeared in the garden in a visible form because He wanted Adam and Eve to know Him (Genesis 3:8). These appearances show the intense desire in the heart of God that we should know Him, not only as our Creator, but also as our friend.

At the heart of the Bible story, God became a man in Jesus Christ. So it should not seem strange that in the Old Testament we find God making these appearances in visible form. It is almost as if the Son of God could not wait to come.

A plunge to disaster

God gave Adam and Eve a single command:

> "But of the tree of the knowledge of good and evil you shall not eat, for in the day that you eat of it you shall surely die."
> (Genesis 2:17)

Adam and Eve already knew about good, and God wanted to protect them from evil. So this command was a wonderful expression of God's love.

The source of all evil was an enemy who came into the garden in the form of a serpent. He questioned God's command, dismissed God's warning, and lured Eve with the enticing prospect of becoming her own god. Adam and Eve disobeyed the command of God. They ate from the tree of the knowledge of good and evil, and in that act of disobedience, they got the knowledge of evil. We have all lived with it ever since.

This first act of disobedience, which the Bible calls sin, led to a great catastrophe.

> He [God] drove out the man, and at the east of the garden of
> Eden he placed the cherubim and a flaming sword that turned
> every way to guard the way to the tree of life. (Genesis 3:24)

Driven from the garden, Adam and Eve found themselves in a very different world in which pain, conflict, frustration, and death were woven into their experience. They were excluded from paradise, and there was no way back. But before they were sent out, God gave the first man and woman hope through a curse and a promise.

The promise of a deliverer

Before driving Adam from the garden, God cursed the serpent. "Cursed are you . . ." (Genesis 3:14). In pronouncing this curse, God was consigning evil to destruction. Evil will not stand. It will be destroyed.

Then God turned to Adam and said, "Cursed . . ." Adam must have held his breath. God had cursed the serpent, and now it seemed He was about to curse Adam too. But instead of saying to Adam, "Cursed are you," God said, "Cursed is the ground because of you" (Genesis 3:17). What did the ground do wrong?

The cursing of the ground tells us something very wonderful about God. He will always deal with sin and destroy it. But God can deflect His judgment away from us, creating room for us to be reconciled to Him.

After God cursed the ground, He promised that a deliverer would come. He said to the serpent:

> "I will put enmity between you and the woman,
>   and between your offspring and her offspring;
> he shall bruise your head,
>   and you shall bruise his heel." (Genesis 3:15)

The rest of the Old Testament is all about this deliverer. It tells us what we need to know to discover who He is, what He has done, and how we can share in the blessing He brings.

From Adam's story we learn who God is. God is our creator. He owns everything, and we belong to Him. God is good and all that is good in our lives and in our world is a loving gift from His hand.

We also learn who we are. We are made in the image of God, and we are made from the dust of the ground. Every human life has unique dignity and worth and every person depends on God for everything.

Adam's story also helps us to understand why our world is so troubled. All that is sad and all that is bad in your life and in the world can be traced back to the catastrophe of Adam's rebellion against God. Adam's sin opened the door to evil, and led to his (and therefore our) exclusion from paradise. War, greed, hatred, and violence are all effects of evil in the world. Drought, earthquakes, sickness, and death are all effects of the curse.

This is the beginning of the Bible story, but it is not the end.

God has promised that someone born of a woman will triumph over evil.

QUESTIONS FOR REFLECTION AND DISCUSSION

What is your first reaction to hearing that we are made in the image of God?

What do you think you would like most about living in the garden of Eden? Why did you choose that?

Does it surprise you to hear that God wants us to know Him? Why or why not?

What is your reaction to the consequences of Adam and Eve's disobedience? Why do you think you reacted that way?

After hearing God's explanation of why our world is so troubled, what kind of deliverer do you think our world needs? What would this deliverer need to do?

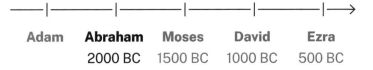

Adam	**Abraham**	Moses	David	Ezra
	2000 BC	1500 BC	1000 BC	500 BC

After Adam and Eve were evicted from the garden, the human
family grew, and as it did, evil and violence increased.
Human rebellion against God continued and increased in the
generations that followed, and God saw that "the wickedness
of man was great in the earth, and that every intention of the
thoughts of his heart was only evil continually" (Genesis 6:5).
God restrained evil by sending a flood, and by confusing
human language. But then God stepped into human history
and revealed Himself to a man called Abraham.

2

ABRAHAM

ABRAHAM WAS BORN about 2,000 years before Jesus and grew up in Mesopotamia, in modern day Iraq. One day God appeared to Abraham as He had appeared to Adam and Eve in the garden.

> "The God of glory appeared to our father Abraham when he was in Mesopotamia, before he lived in Haran." (Acts 7:2)

You might think that a man to whom God would appear in visible form must have been especially holy. Precisely the opposite was the case. Abraham worshiped idols (Joshua 24:2). So, God took the initiative and made Himself known to Abraham. It is almost as if God had said, "If I wait for these human beings to seek me, they will never come. I will seek them, I will find them, and I will bless them." God was looking for Abraham long before Abraham was looking for God, and God seeks us before we seek Him.

A promise given

When God appeared to Abraham, He gave a marvelous promise.

> "I will bless you ... and in you all the families of the earth shall be blessed." (Genesis 12:2, 3)

The promise to Abraham is a promise for us and for every member of the human family. The Old Testament focuses on the line of Abraham, not because the rest of the world doesn't matter, but because the rest of the world does matter, and God's plan is to bless all the families of the earth through Abraham.

Notice again the abundant goodness of God. We have turned away from God and put our own gods or our own choices in the place that belongs to Him. Evil has multiplied across the human family as generations have rebelled against God, and yet God's desire is to bless not just some but all the families of the earth.

But how would God's blessing come?

God promised that His blessing would come through Abraham's offspring (Genesis 22:18). But Abraham was an old man, and he had no descendant, so how could this promise be fulfilled?

Years passed and Abraham waited. His wife, Sarah, laughed when God promised her a child (Genesis 18:12). But God is always true to His word, and sure enough, in her old age Sarah gave birth to Isaac (Genesis 21:2–3). Every child is precious, but after waiting so long for a child on whom so much would depend, Isaac was Abraham and Sarah's greatest treasure.

A promise fulfilled

God's promise to bless all people would be fulfilled at an unimaginable cost, and that cost is illustrated by the harrowing story of how God tested Abraham.

> He said, "Take your son, your only son Isaac, whom you love, and go to the land of Moriah, and offer him there as a burnt offering on one of the mountains of which I shall tell you." (Genesis 22:2)

Abraham never questioned the need for a sacrifice. He seems to have understood that if God's blessing was to reach the nations of the world, some great sacrifice would be needed.

Try and put yourself in Abraham's shoes. What would you have done?

Abraham must have wrestled with what God told him to do. "God has called me to make the ultimate sacrifice, but how can I give up my son? God's plan is to bring blessing to all people, but how can that happen if I don't do what He says? God's promise is to bless the world through my offspring, but how can the promise be fulfilled if Isaac dies? And what in the world would I say to Sarah?"

Whatever battles Abraham went through, he chose to obey God.

> And Abraham took the wood of the burnt offering and laid it on Isaac his son. And he took in his hand the fire and the knife. So they went both of them together. And Isaac said to his father Abraham, "My father!" And he said, "Here I am, my son." He said, "Behold, the fire and the wood, but where is the lamb for

a burnt offering?" Abraham said, "God will provide for himself the lamb for a burnt offering, my son." So they went both of them together. (Genesis 22:6–8)

Isaac was in the prime of his life. He carried the wood on his shoulders, and he could easily have overpowered Abraham, if he had wanted to. But Isaac didn't do that. He was willing to lay down his life. So, what you have here is a father willing to give up his son, and a son who is willing to give himself. And they were *one* in this, so that blessing would come to the world.

When they arrived at the top of the mountain, Abraham built an altar.

Then Abraham reached out his hand and took the knife to slaughter his son. But the angel of the Lord called to him from heaven and said, "Abraham, Abraham! . . . Do not lay your hand on the boy or do anything to him." (Genesis 22:10–12)

God tested Abraham, but He would not allow Abraham to give up his son. God provided the sacrifice, as Abraham said He would.

Abraham lifted up his eyes and looked, and behold, behind him was a ram, caught in a thicket by his horns. And Abraham went and took the ram and offered it up as a burnt offering instead of his son. (Genesis 22:13)

The ram was a *substitute* for Isaac. Isaac's life was spared because the ram took his place on the altar. The life of a ram was of far less value than the life of Isaac, but God accepted a lesser sacrifice for the time being because one day a greater sacrifice would be made. Abraham must have wondered, *What will it cost for God's blessing to come to the world? What sacrifice could be greater than the sacrifice of my son?*

We are meant to respond to this story in two ways: First, I hope you will feel a sense of recoiling in horror at the thought of anyone sacrificing his own son. That is what you are meant to feel.

Second, I hope you will gaze in wonder at the reality to which this story points. God did what He would not allow Abraham to do. He gave His Son, and His Son gave Himself. God's promise to bring blessing to all the families of the earth came through His Son Jesus, and it came at unimaginable cost to both the Father and the Son.

QUESTIONS FOR REFLECTION AND DISCUSSION

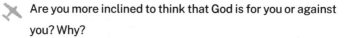 What is your first reaction to hearing that God seeks us before we seek Him?

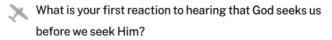 Are you more inclined to think that God is for you or against you? Why?

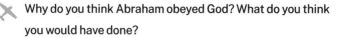 What signs of God's blessing can you see in your life?

Why do you think Abraham obeyed God? What do you think you would have done?

Have you ever felt that God was testing you? How did you respond?

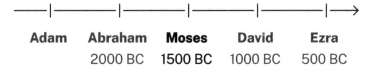

| Adam | Abraham | **Moses** | David | Ezra |
| | 2000 BC | **1500 BC** | 1000 BC | 500 BC |

Abraham's son Isaac became the father of Jacob, who had twelve sons. Jacob's family moved to Egypt where they found food in a time of famine, and their descendants remained there for 400 years. The family God had promised to bless multiplied, but as their numbers grew, they were oppressed. They cried out to God and He answered their prayer by sending Moses.

3

MOSES

MOSES' LIFE WAS IN DANGER from the moment he was born. In a despicable act of ethnic cleansing, Pharaoh instructed his people to throw every male child descended from Abraham into the Nile river (Exodus 1:22). But Moses' mother came up with a plan to save her son. She put him in a basket and hid him in the reeds at the edge of the river.

One day, Pharaoh's daughter came down to the river to bathe. She found the basket and, taking pity on the infant inside, she brought Moses home and raised him in the palace. Moses grew up surrounded by every luxury money could buy, but he knew that he did not belong in the palace. He belonged to the line of Abraham, and his people were in trouble. So, he left the palace and identified himself with the people God had promised to bless.

God commissioned Moses to bring His people out of Egypt and lead them into the land He had promised (Genesis 12:7). By this time, the descendants of Abraham numbered 600,000 men (Exodus 12:37), so the entire community would have been about two million people.

These men were Pharoah's workforce, so at first, he refused to let them leave. But after a series of plagues that God sent through Moses, he relented and let God's people go (Exodus 12:31). But, after they left, Pharaoh changed his mind again and sent his armies after them.

When the people came to the Red Sea, it seemed that they were trapped. But God made a path for them through the sea.

> Then Moses stretched out his hand over the sea, and the LORD drove the sea back by a strong east wind all night and made the sea dry land, and the waters were divided. And the people of Israel went into the midst of the sea on dry ground, the waters being a wall to them on their right hand and on their left. (Exodus 14:21–22)

But when the pursuing army tried to cross, God caused the wall of water to collapse over them. God's people knew that they had been saved from certain destruction by a miracle that only God Himself could have performed.

God gave Moses the Ten Commandments

After this great deliverance, Moses led the people to Mount Sinai where God gave them the Ten Commandments.

And God spoke all these words, saying,

"I am the LORD your God, who brought you out of the land of Egypt, out of the house of slavery."

1. You shall have no other gods before me.

2. You shall not make for yourself a carved image, or any likeness of anything that is in heaven above, or that is in the earth beneath, or that is in the water under the earth.

3. You shall not take the name of the LORD your God in vain.

4. Remember the Sabbath day, to keep it holy. Six days you shall labor, and do all your work, but the seventh day is a Sabbath to the LORD your God.

5. Honor your father and your mother, that your days may be long in the land that the LORD your God is giving you.

6. You shall not murder.

7. You shall not commit adultery.

8. You shall not steal.

9. You shall not bear false witness against your neighbor.

10. You shall not covet your neighbor's house; you shall not covet your neighbor's wife, or his male servant, or his female servant, or his ox, or his donkey, or anything that is your neighbor's." (See Exodus 20:1–17)

These commandments are a direct reflection of the character of God, and God calls His people to live a life that reflects who He is. Why should you not commit adultery? Because God is faithful. Why should you not steal? Because God can be trusted. Why should you not lie? Because God's Word is truth.

The Ten Commandments also spell out what it means to love. The first four commands tell us what it looks like to love God. Loving God involves putting Him first, embracing Him as He is, honoring His name, and giving Him time. The last six commands tell us what it looks like to love our neighbor. Loving others involves giving honor where honor is due, acting in the best interest of others, being faithful, giving rather than taking, telling the truth, and rejoicing in what God has given to others.

God gave Moses the sacrifices

A world where these commands are always fulfilled would be supremely good. But while Moses was receiving the Ten Commandments at the top of the mountain, God's people were breaking them at the bottom of the mountain.

In Moses' absence, his brother, Aaron, made a golden idol in the shape of a calf, and the people said, "These are your gods, O Israel, who brought you up out of the land of Egypt" (Exodus 32:4). So, God said to Moses, "Go down, for your people, whom you brought up out of the land of Egypt, have corrupted themselves" (Exodus 32:7).

God's people had broken the first commandment. Moses

called them to repent, and the vast majority of them did. But something more was needed before they could be forgiven. An offense had been committed and a price would have to be paid. According to Hebrews 9:22, "Without the shedding of blood there is no forgiveness of sins."

When God gave the laws, He also gave the sacrifices to His people. Forgiveness and restoration were always in the mind and the heart of God, and the sacrifices meant that God's people were saved from facing the full penalties of the law.

Even at this early stage in the Bible story, God is preparing us for the coming of Jesus. The sacrifices in the Old Testament show why the Son of God had to come into the world. Jesus did what the sacrifice of animals could only point to. He made atonement for our sins, and forgiveness is found through faith in Him.

QUESTIONS FOR REFLECTION AND DISCUSSION

 What is your first reaction when you hear that God saved His people by parting the Red Sea?

 Which commandment seems the most relevant to your life right now? Why?

Which command sounds the most challenging to you? Why?

 How can people be forgiven if they break the Ten Commandments?

Would you like to live in a world where everyone followed the Ten Commandments?

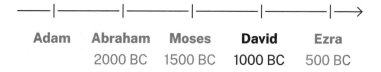

Adam	Abraham	Moses	David	Ezra
	2000 BC	1500 BC	1000 BC	500 BC

After Moses died, God brought His people into the Promised Land under the leadership of Joshua. What followed was a long period of chaos in which God's people kept turning away from Him. When they disobeyed God, He allowed their enemies to prevail over them. When they turned back to God, He raised up leaders called judges to deliver them. But when the judge died, God's people turned away from Him, and the whole cycle started over again.

4

DAVID

OTHER NATIONS had a settled form of leadership and God's people wanted to have a king. The first king, whose name was Saul, was a big disappointment. He was arrogant, devious, and foolish, and over time, he became increasingly unstable. God had another king in mind who would reflect His own heart, and at the direction of the Lord, David was anointed by Samuel the prophet (1 Samuel 16:13). But years would pass before David came to the throne.

David got people's attention when they heard the story of his great victory over Goliath. This giant of a man was nine feet tall, his armor weighed 125 pounds, and he carried a long javelin with an iron point.

Every morning Goliath came out to taunt the people of God.

"Choose a man for yourselves, and let him come down to me.
If he is able to fight with me and kill me, then we will be your

> servants. But if I prevail against him and kill him, then you shall
> be our servants and serve us." (1 Samuel 17:8–9)

The Israelites didn't know what to do. They all felt that they would be losers against Goliath. So the taunts and the humiliation went on, until David arrived and offered to fight him.

David must have looked pitifully small as he faced up to the giant on the other side of the valley. But Goliath had defied God and God was with David.

> David put his hand in his bag and took out a stone and slung it
> and struck the Philistine on his forehead. The stone sank into his
> forehead, and he fell on his face to the ground. (1 Samuel 17:49)

David's victory gives us a window into the central Bible story. A thousand years after the time of David, Jesus, a descendent of King David, arrived on the field of battle and faced up to our greatest enemies. If Jesus had lost, there would have been no hope for us. But Jesus triumphed over our greatest enemies—sin, death, and hell—and all of His people will share in His victory.

David was without question the greatest of the Old Testament kings. Under his leadership, the twelve tribes of Israel were united as one people. Enemies who had oppressed the people of God were pushed back and God's people prospered. With strong defense, a thriving economy, and stable leadership, God's people had never had it so good.

We need a better king

David was a strong-willed and impulsive man who accomplished great things, but he also had some great failures. Sometimes we learn from him by example. Other times we learn from him by contrast.

David abused his power and committed adultery with a woman called Bathsheba. When she became pregnant David recalled her husband, Uriah, who was serving in the king's army, and sent him home so that when the child was born, Uriah and everyone else would assume that this was his child. But Uriah was a man of honor. He refused to enjoy the comforts of home while the men with whom he served were risking their lives on the field of battle.

So David sent Uriah back to the battle with a sealed letter of instruction to his commander:

> "Set Uriah in the forefront of the hardest fighting, and then draw back from him, that he may be struck down, and die."
> (2 Samuel 11:15)

The news of Uriah's death was reported to Bathsheba, and after a period of mourning, David sent for her, and she became his wife. The cover up was complete, except for one thing: God knew. "The thing that David had done displeased the LORD" (2 Samuel 11:27).

David had defied God's commandments. He had coveted his neighbor's wife, he had lied to Bathsheba and Uriah, he had stolen another man's wife, he had committed adultery, and he had taken another man's life.

God sent the prophet Nathan to confront David over his secret sin. He told David a story about a rich man who stole a lamb from a poor man to feed a guest who had come to his home. David, who as king was responsible for justice in the land, was outraged when he heard this story.

> Then David's anger was greatly kindled against the man, and he said to Nathan, "As the LORD lives, the man who has done this deserves to die." (2 Samuel 12:5)

Then Nathan said to David, "You are the man!" (v. 7).

And David said, "I have sinned against the LORD" (v. 13).

The way of the sinner is hard. David experienced deep pain in his own family that reflected the pain caused to others by his own sin. But David walked the way of a repentant sinner, and God walked this hard road with him (see Psalm 51). Any road, however hard, that is walked with God is better by far than the easiest road walked without Him.

Despite all his achievements, David's story points us to our need for a better king. The contrast between David and Jesus is striking. David gave up the life of Uriah to save himself. But Jesus gave up His own life to save others.

God gave David a promise

David wanted to build a temple to honor God, but God had other plans and He announced them in a stunning promise.

"I will raise up your offspring after you . . . and I will establish his kingdom. He shall build a house for my name, and I will establish the throne of his kingdom forever. I will be to him a father, and he shall be to me a son." (2 Samuel 7:12–14)

The Bible story is about how God's blessing will come to all people. God had already promised that His blessing would come through a descendant of Abraham. Now, a thousand years later, God revealed that it would come through a king in the line of David.

When we come to the New Testament, the very first verse says,

The book of the genealogy of Jesus Christ, the son of David, the son of Abraham. (Matthew 1:1)

Jesus is the One in whom God's promises to Abraham and to David are fulfilled. He's the One in whom all the families of the earth will be blessed. He is the King who will reign forever. He was born into the line of David, but God is His Father and He is God's Son.

QUESTIONS FOR REFLECTION
AND DISCUSSION

 What is your first reaction to King David's sin with Bathsheba?

 Do you agree that sin, death, and hell are our greatest enemies? Why?

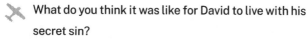 What do you think it was like for David to live with his secret sin?

If you had a secret sin, would you want God to send someone like Nathan to you? Why or why not?

Have you ever wanted to do something for God, but He closed the door on your good intentions?

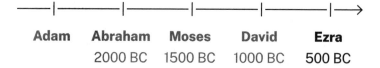

Adam   **Abraham**   **Moses**   **David**   **Ezra**
2000 BC   1500 BC   1000 BC   500 BC

After the time of David, God's people turned to other gods,
and after the reign of his son Solomon, the kingdom divided
in two. Ten tribes in the north declared independence from the
line of David. There were nineteen kings in the north, and
all of them did evil in the eyes of the Lord. Then the northern
kingdom collapsed, and its people were scattered.

5

EZRA

TWO TRIBES IN THE SOUTH continued under kings in the line of David. Most of these kings led the people to worship other gods, and this idolatry was so offensive to God that He gave His people into the hands of their enemies.

The king of Babylon laid siege to the city of Jerusalem and reduced it to a pile of rubble. The temple was destroyed, and those who survived were taken into exile in Babylon. The books of Ezekiel, Daniel, and Lamentations were all written during this dark time. But God always keeps His promises, and even in this darkest hour, there was still hope for God's people.

> But this I call to mind,
>> and therefore I have hope:
>
> The steadfast love of the LORD never ceases;
>> his mercies never come to an end;

they are new every morning;

　great is your faithfulness.

"The Lᴏʀᴅ is my portion," says my soul,

　"therefore I will hope in him." (Lamentations 3:21–24)

Seventy years after God's people were taken into exile, Babylon fell to the rising empire of the Medes and the Persians. The new king, Cyrus, decreed that any Jewish exiles who wished to return to Jerusalem were free to do so, and a group of about fifty thousand people caught the vision of creating a new community in the city of God.

Most of God's people remained in exile, but eighty years later, Ezra led a second group of exiles back to Jerusalem. Ezra was a priest and a scribe, and God's hand was on him in a special way:

He [Ezra] came to Jerusalem, for the good hand of his God was on him. (Ezra 7:9)

I took courage, for the hand of the Lᴏʀᴅ my God was on me, and I gathered leading men from Israel to go up with me. (Ezra 7:28)

The hand of our God was on us, and he delivered us from the hand of the enemy and from ambushes by the way. (Ezra 8:31)

Ezra's story is not primarily about what he did for God, but what God did through him.

Restoring God's people

When Ezra arrived in Jerusalem, he found that God's people had adopted the detestable, idolatrous practices of the surrounding nations (Ezra 9:1–4). Ezra tore his clothes, pulled out his hair, and cried out:

> "O my God, I am ashamed and blush to lift my face to you, my God, for our iniquities have risen higher than our heads, and our guilt has mounted up to the heavens. . . . And now, O our God, what shall we say after this? For we have forsaken your commandments." (Ezra 9:6, 10)

Eighty years after the first exiles returned to Jerusalem, their grandchildren had lost sight of their distinct calling to worship and serve the Lord. But God used Ezra to lead a great restoration among His people.

> The good hand of his God was on him. For Ezra had set his heart to study the Law of the LORD, and to do it and to teach his statutes and rules in Israel. (Ezra 7:9–10)

God's hand was on Ezra as he studied and obeyed the Scriptures, and God's hand will be on you when the Word of God is in you.

Ezra's strategy for restoring God's people was to gather them around God's Word:

> So Ezra the priest brought the Law before the assembly, both men and women and all who could understand what they heard. (Nehemiah 8:2)

The Levites supported him by reading, explaining, and applying the Word of God:

> They read from the book, from the Law of God, clearly, and they gave the sense, so that the people understood the reading. (Nehemiah 8:8)

The first response of God's people was to weep because they saw how far they were from fulfilling God's commands: "All the people wept as they heard the words of the Law" (Nehemiah 8:9).

When the light of God's Word comes into our lives, we begin to see how far we are from Him, and we feel our own need. So don't be surprised if your first reaction to opening the Bible is to feel your own unworthiness. God's Word will bring you there, but it will never leave you there.

Then Ezra said, "Do not be grieved, for the joy of the LORD is your strength" (Nehemiah 8:10). Opening the Bible brings great joy because, from beginning to end, the Bible is good news. God's people didn't go home preoccupied with their sins and failures. When the Bible was opened, they discovered the grace and mercy of God, and this gave them strength.

Still waiting

From the stories of Adam, Abraham, Moses, David, and Ezra, we have seen that God was constantly at work. He raised up many prophets who spoke His Word, many priests who offered prayers and sacrifices on behalf of the people, and many kings who led the people in triumph. But despite all their efforts, little had changed.

God's people kept turning away from Him, and God kept calling them back. In the last book of the Old Testament, God says,

> "From the days of your fathers you have turned aside from my statutes and have not kept them. Return to me, and I will return to you, says the Lord of hosts." (Malachi 3:7)

The curse God had pronounced in the garden of Eden was still hanging over His people.

> "You are cursed with a curse, for you are robbing me, the whole nation of you." (Malachi 3:9)

And God's people were still waiting.

> "For still the vision awaits its appointed time;
>   it hastens to the end — it will not lie.
> If it seems slow, wait for it;
>   it will surely come; it will not delay." (Habakkuk 2:3)

But God had promised that a deliverer would come.

> Rejoice greatly, O daughter of Zion!
>   Shout aloud, O daughter of Jerusalem!
> Behold, your king is coming to you;
>   righteous and having salvation is he. (Zechariah 9:9)

God's promise was fulfilled when Jesus Christ was born. The Old Testament explains why we need Him. The New Testament tells us what happened when He came.

QUESTIONS FOR REFLECTION AND DISCUSSION

 What is your first reaction to God giving His people into the hands of their enemies?

 Have you sensed God's hand of blessing on your life as you open the Bible? If so, how?

 Is there something in the Bible that has troubled you or made you feel unworthy? If so, what was it?

 Where have you seen the clearest glimpses of the grace and kindness of God?

From what you learned from the Old Testament, why do you think we need a deliverer? Do you think that you need a deliverer?

PART 2

FIVE EVENTS IN THE LIFE OF JESUS

Born   **Tempted**   **Crucified**   **Risen**   **Ascended**

30 years   3 years   3 days   40 days

The five people we looked at in the Old Testament all point to one person, Jesus Christ. The whole Bible story is about Him, and we learn about His life in the Gospels — Matthew, Mark, Luke, and John. We will look at five events in the life of Jesus: He was born, He was tempted, He was crucified, He is risen, and He has ascended. We begin with the birth of Jesus.

6

BORN

THE BIRTH OF JESUS was the first evidence that He is unlike any other person who has ever lived. This is how it came about: Mary was a young woman preparing for marriage to a man named Joseph. God spoke to her through an angel, who appeared to her and said,

> "Do not be afraid, Mary, for you have found favor with God. And behold, you will conceive in your womb and bear a son, and you shall call his name Jesus." (Luke 1:30–31)

Mary was a virgin, so she asked, "How will this be?" (v. 34). The angel's answer takes us to the heart of a wonderful mystery.

> "The Holy Spirit will come upon you, and the power of the Most High will overshadow you; therefore the child to be born will be called holy — the Son of God." (Luke 1:35)

Mary could not have understood all that the angel said to her but, in an act of faith, she submitted herself to God's plan: "Behold, I am the servant of the Lord; let it be to me according to your word" (Luke 1:38).

Shortly before the birth of Jesus, Caesar Augustus issued a decree requiring everyone in the country to register in the place where they were born. This meant that Mary and Joseph had to travel to Bethlehem. All the inns in the little town were already full, so Mary and Joseph found a place of shelter with the animals, and it was there that Jesus was born.

> And she gave birth to her firstborn son and wrapped him in swaddling cloths and laid him in a manger, because there was no place for them in the inn. (Luke 2:7)

Jesus is Savior and King

The world might have missed the birth of Jesus, except for two events.

First, an angel appeared to shepherds and said,

> "Fear not, for behold, I bring you good news of great joy that will be for all the people. For unto you is born this day in the city of David a Savior, who is Christ the Lord." (Luke 2:10–11)

The shepherds rushed to Bethlehem where they found Mary, Joseph, and the baby, and after their visit, they told the good news they had received to everyone they could.

Those who heard what they said "wondered at what the shepherds told them" (Luke 2:18). *What if this is true?* That's a good place to begin. If God has sent a Savior, then there is hope for you. You can have peace with God. Your sins and failings are not the end. You can be forgiven. You can be rescued.

Second, wise men from the East followed a star that appeared when Jesus was born. When they came to Jerusalem, they asked:

> "Where is he who has been born king of the Jews? For we saw his star when it rose and have come to worship him." (Matthew 2:2)

These wise men were likely kings, and they recognized the authority of Jesus over them. Jesus is the King and even kings worshiped Him.

So, what does it mean for Jesus to be the King? It means that He has the right to direct what we believe and how we live. But while kings from the East worshiped Him, King Herod was so determined to destroy Him that he ordered the killing of all the male children in Bethlehem and the surrounding region.

People are still divided over Jesus. Some trust Him as Savior and worship Him as king; others see no need of His salvation and defy Him by resisting His rule over their lives. It has been so since the moment of His birth.

So why does Jesus have the right to rule over every life?

Jesus is God

The angel announced to Mary that her child would be "the Son of God" (Luke 1:35). Then, in a separate appearance to Joseph, Jesus was announced as *Immanuel*, which means "God with us" (Matthew 1:23).

Mary was a virgin, and her child was born as the result of a direct initiative of God. Joseph made no contribution whatsoever. The life in Mary's womb came to be there through a creative work of the Holy Spirit. God did not wait for a deliverer to arise *from* the human race. He came *to* the human race. God became a man, taking flesh from Mary.

Your life began when you were conceived in your mother's womb. Before that moment you did not exist. But with Jesus, it was different. His life did not begin in Mary's womb. Before He was born in the stable, He shared the life of God in heaven.

Jesus has always shared the Father's glory and the Father's love (John 17:5, 24), but

> though he was in the form of God, [he] did not count equality with God a thing to be grasped, but emptied himself, by taking the form of a servant, being born in the likeness of men.
> (Philippians 2:6–7)

Jesus is a man

We'll never be able to fully understand how God could take human flesh and be born as a baby, but the central claim of the New Testament is that He did. And this is what qualifies Him to be our Savior.

Picture a mediator between two alienated parties. He places one arm around the one who has been offended and the other arm around the one who has caused the offense and brings the two together. Jesus is that mediator between God and us (1 Timothy 2:5). Jesus is able to save us because He is one with God and one with us.

The miracle of how God became a man is an unfathomable mystery, but it makes sense of everything else the Bible tells us about Jesus. If God became a man in Jesus, then His claims, His miracles, and His resurrection should bring no surprise. The incarnation is the mystery that makes sense of everything else.

QUESTIONS FOR REFLECTION AND DISCUSSION

 What is your first reaction to hearing that Jesus was born of a virgin?

 The angels said that the birth of Jesus is good news of great joy for all people. Does it sound like good news to you?

 People are still divided over Jesus. What reactions to Him have you seen?

 Do you feel a tension or division in your heart about Jesus? Why do you think that might be?

 Do you think that Jesus has the right to rule over your life? Why or why not?

Born   **Tempted**   **Crucified**   **Risen**   **Ascended**

30 years   3 years   3 days   40 days

The birth of Jesus must have set alarm bells ringing in hell. The presence of light spells the end for darkness, and God's immediate presence on earth as a man would lead to the destruction of evil — unless Satan could find a way to destroy Jesus. His first attempt came through the rage of King Herod, whose murder of innocent children was an intolerable crime. But when that dark deed failed, Satan was forced out into the open in a direct confrontation with Jesus.

7

TEMPTED

JESUS WAS 30 years of age when He began His public ministry. He was baptized in the river Jordan, identifying Himself fully with men and women who seek to live for the glory of God. The Holy Spirit descended on Jesus, and an audible voice from heaven said, "This is my beloved Son, with whom I am well pleased" (Matthew 3:17).

Filled with the Holy Spirit, Jesus went into the desert, where He endured a period of intense temptation that lasted for forty days. It is significant that the Spirit led Jesus into the desert (Luke 4:1). He was stalking the enemy. He had come into the world to destroy Satan's work, and the first step in His public ministry was to confront our enemy and triumph where Adam had failed.

Confusion, presumption, and ambition

Satan appears to have a limited number of strategies. This is evident from the parallels between his successful tempting of Adam and Eve in the garden and his total failure to compromise the integrity of the Lord Jesus Christ in the desert.

Satan's first strategy in the garden was an attempt to create confusion about what God had said. He asked Eve, "Did God actually say, 'You shall not eat of any tree in the garden'?" (Genesis 3:1). In the desert, the enemy tried to create confusion about Jesus' identity. "If you are the Son of God," he said, "command these stones to become loaves of bread" (Matthew 4:3). But Jesus did not need to perform a miracle to prove that He was, and is, the Son of God. He answered, "It is written, 'Man shall not live by bread alone, but by every word that comes from the mouth of God'" (Matthew 4:4).

His second strategy in the garden was an attempt to promote presumption. Satan tried to convince Eve that she could disobey the command of God without consequence. "You will not surely die," he said (Genesis 3:4). He used the same line of argument when he dared Jesus to throw Himself down from the highest point of the temple, with the promise that God would send an angel to catch Him. Such a spectacular display would surely get people's attention. But Jesus knew the difference between faith and presumption: "Again it is written, 'You shall not put the Lord your God to the test'" (Matthew 4:7).

The third strategy centered on ambition. Satan promised Eve that asserting her independence would put her in a position of equality with God. "You will be like God," he said (Genesis 3:5). Having succeeded with this strategy once, the enemy tried the same approach against Jesus, saying in essence, "Worship me and I will give you all the glory of the kingdoms of the world" (Luke 4:5–7). But Jesus said, "Be gone, Satan! For it is written, 'You shall worship the Lord your God and him only shall you serve'" (Matthew 4:10).

Satan launched everything he had in his assault against Jesus, but he could not break Him. And after he had exhausted every strategy he knew, he was left with no alternative but to retreat.

The full force of the enemy

Only Jesus knows the full power of temptation because only Jesus has withstood the full force of the enemy's assault.

Imagine three airmen flying jets over enemy territory during a war. They are shot down, captured, and then taken by the enemy for interrogation. One by one they are brought into a darkened room.

The first airman gives his name, rank, and serial number. His captors ask him for the position of his forces. He knows that he must not give this information, but he also knows that the enemy is cruel. So he tells them what he knows.

The second airman is brought in, and they begin to question him. He is determined not to give in. So the cruelty begins and eventually it overwhelms him. He breaks and tells them what he knows.

Then the third airman comes in. "You will not break me," he says. "Oh yes, we will. We have broken every man who has ever come into this room. It is only a matter of time; you'll see."

The cruelty begins, but he does not break. So it is intensified, and then it is intensified more, until it feels unbearable, but still he does not break.

Finally, there comes a point when they have tried everything they know. "It's no use," they say. "He is not like any other person we've had in this room. We can't break him."

Which of these airmen faced the full force of the enemy? The only one to know the full force of the enemy's assault is the one who did not break. So don't ever think that Jesus' temptations were less than yours. Jesus knows the full power of temptation because Jesus has withstood the full force of the enemy's assault.

Jesus is able to help you when you are tempted. He understands your temptations, because He Himself has been tempted, and He can give you the strength you need to prevail in your battle (Hebrews 4:15–16).

The promised deliverer

Jesus returned from the desert in the power of the Holy Spirit to begin His public ministry. In the synagogue at Nazareth, He read the words of Isaiah the prophet about the promised deliverer:

"The Spirit of the Lord is upon me,

because he has anointed me

to proclaim good news to the poor.

He has sent me to proclaim liberty to the captives

and recovering of sight to the blind,

to set at liberty those who are oppressed,

to proclaim the year of the Lord's favor." (Luke 4:18–19)

Jesus rolled up the scroll, gave it to the attendant, and sat down. The eyes of everyone were on Him, waiting for what He would say: "Today," Jesus announced, "this Scripture has been fulfilled in your hearing" (Luke 4:21). You might think that the people would welcome God's promised deliverer, but the response of these people was to drive Him out of their town (Luke 4:29).

What followed was three years in which Jesus gave Himself to serving God by serving others. His disciples witnessed His power over nature, as He calmed a storm; over demons, as He released the oppressed; over disease, as He healed the sick; and even over the grave, as He raised the dead. Many believed and followed Him, but there was also relentless opposition, which ultimately led to His arrest, trial, and crucifixion.

QUESTIONS FOR REFLECTION
AND DISCUSSION

 What is your first reaction to the temptations of Jesus?

 Have you ever felt that you were being tempted? Did that temptation involve confusion, presumption, or ambition?

 To which of Satan's strategies do you feel most vulnerable? Why?

 On a scale of 1 (not much help at all) to 10 (all the help I need), how much help do you think Jesus could be to you in your temptations? Why did you answer the way you did?

 How do you think people would react in your town if Jesus came and did miracles there today? Why?

Born   **Tempted**   **Crucified**   **Risen**   **Ascended**

30 years   3 years   3 days   40 days

After He was tempted, Jesus engaged in three years of public ministry in which He taught, performed miracles, and called people to follow Him. His message was clear: "Repent, for the kingdom of heaven is at hand" (Matthew 4:17). "Repent and believe in the gospel" (Mark 1:15). Crowds followed Jesus but, from the beginning, the powers of the state and religion opposed Him. And after three years, He was arrested, tried, and condemned to die on a cross.

8

CRUCIFIED

JESUS WAS ARRESTED by Roman soldiers, surrounded by a mob armed with swords and clubs. Then, in the course of a single night, He was dragged from one trial to another—before the high priest, the king, and Pontius Pilate. As the Roman governor, Pilate pronounced Jesus innocent, but under pressure from the crowd, he had Jesus scourged. When the crowd was not satisfied, he handed Jesus over to be crucified (John 19:16).

What must have gone through the minds of angels as they watched what was happening on that cross? They had gasped in wonder when they saw the Son of God take human flesh as He was born into the world. Now they saw that flesh torn by a whip, a crown of thorns being embedded in His head, and nails piercing His hands and feet.

Man's sin reached its full horror and its most awful expression at the cross. We had disobeyed God's commands. Now we were crucifying God's Son. If ever there was a moment in human history when God's judgment had to fall, this was it.

Jesus knew that God's judgment would come, but He cried out, "Father, forgive them, for they do not know what they are doing" (Luke 23:34 NIV). He was saying, "Don't let it fall on them; let it fall on Me. Let Me be the lightning rod for Your judgment on their sin." This is the heart of the gospel. Jesus took the penalty for our sins so that we might be forgiven.

Jesus' prayer, "Father, forgive them," covers the sin of every person who will come to Him. If it could cover the sin of those who nailed Jesus to the cross, it can cover every sin of yours.

Paradise is opened

Two thieves were hanging on crosses, one on either side of Jesus. Having pursued a life of crime, they had faced human justice and were now paying the price. Soon, death would relieve their suffering, but then they would enter the presence of God where they would face divine justice. Their position seemed hopeless.

Both joined the crowd in ridiculing Jesus (Matthew 27:44). But as death drew near, something changed. One of them had a new awareness that soon he would enter the presence of God, and while the other thief continued reviling Jesus, this man rebuked him: "Do you not fear God?" He had heard Jesus praying, "Father, forgive them." Perhaps Jesus could forgive him too.

And He said, "Jesus, remember me when you come into your kingdom." And [Jesus] said to him, "Truly, I say to you, today you will be with me in paradise." (Luke 23:42–43)

Paradise! This man had made a tragic waste of his life, but Jesus promised him an immediate translation, through death, into a life of undiluted joy. Suddenly this man, who had been on the brink of hell found that, because of Jesus, he was about to enter the joy of heaven. Jesus opened the way back to God's presence and blessing, not only for the thief, but for all who will trust in Him.

The sun stopped shining

Jesus had suffered the judgment of men. Now, He would endure the judgment of God, and as He entered into the heart of His sufferings, God kept the sun from shining: "It was now about the sixth hour, and there was darkness over the whole land until the ninth hour" (Luke 23:44).

In these hours of darkness, Jesus bore our guilt and absorbed God's wrath. He endured all this alone, without the comfort of His Father's love, and in the depth of His suffering, He cried out, "My God, my God, why have you forsaken me?" (Mark 15:34).

God tells us what Jesus was doing in that awful darkness:

He himself bore our sins in his body on the tree. (1 Peter 2:24)

He was pierced for our transgressions;

   he was crushed for our iniquities;

upon him was the chastisement that brought us peace,

   and with his wounds we are healed.

All we like sheep have gone astray;

   we have turned — every one — to his own way;

and the LORD has laid on him

   the iniquity of us all. (Isaiah 53:5–6)

These Scriptures, and many more, point to the marvelous truth that God reconciles sinners to Himself through Jesus Christ.

Death is subdued

After three hours, the darkness passed. The judgment poured out on Jesus was exhausted and spent. Justice was satisfied, and Jesus shouted in triumph, "It is finished" (John 19:30).

All that was needed to redeem God's people had been accomplished: Forgiveness was released, condemnation was removed, and heaven was opened for all who would trust in Jesus.

Then Jesus called out with a loud voice, "'Father, into your hands I commit my spirit!' And having said this, he breathed his last" (Luke 23:46). When someone dies, their voice becomes weaker and weaker until they are hardly able to speak. No one speaks in a loud voice at the moment of death. But Jesus did.

Jesus was not overcome by death. He said, "No one takes [my

life] from me, but I lay it down of my own accord. I have authority to lay it down, and I have authority to take it up again" (John 10:17–18). The life of Jesus was given, not taken. He gave Himself for us.

Jesus has changed the nature of death for all who believe. When He died, the judgment and condemnation that was due to us was poured out on Him. "There is therefore now no condemnation for those who are in Christ Jesus" (Romans 8:1).

QUESTIONS FOR REFLECTION AND DISCUSSION

What is your first reaction to Jesus' death on the cross?

Jesus said "Father, forgive them." What do you think you would be saying if you had to endure the suffering and shame of the cross even though you were innocent?

Which thief do you identify with the most — the one who was shouting at Jesus? Or the one who asked Jesus to remember him? Why?

How would you explain why Jesus died on the cross to a friend who asked you?

Is there anything in your life that might keep you from dying as confidently as Jesus did?

Born   **Tempted**   **Crucified**   **Risen**   **Ascended**

30 years   3 years   **3 days**   40 days

Jesus was given an honored burial. Joseph of Arimathea, a respected member of the Jewish ruling council, asked Pilate for the body of Jesus and, assisted by Nicodemus, he took the body down from the cross and prepared it for burial. Together, they laid it in a tomb and rolled a large stone in front of the entrance. Pilate then ordered that the tomb should be sealed and guarded. But on the third day, the tomb was empty.

9

RISEN

IT IS HARD TO BE CERTAIN of the exact order of events on Easter morning because each of the Gospel writers focuses on different aspects of the story.

Early in the morning, a group of women went to the tomb to pack spices around the body of Jesus (Luke 24:1). They knew that the tomb had been sealed with a stone and they were wondering who might help them to get in (Mark 16:3). But when they arrived, they found that the stone had been rolled away and that the tomb was empty (Luke 24:2–3).

Mary Magdalene was so distressed that she left the other women at the tomb and ran to tell Peter and John, "They have taken the Lord out of the tomb, and we do not know where they have laid him" (John 20:2).

When Peter heard this news, he ran to the tomb and, finding it empty, he "went away, wondering to himself what had happened"

(Luke 24:12 NIV). The other disciples seem to have had a similar reaction. When they first heard that Jesus had risen, "these words seemed to them an idle tale, and they did not believe them" (Luke 24:11).

While Mary Magdalene was gone, an angel appeared to the women who remained at the tomb, and said,

> "Do not be alarmed. You seek Jesus of Nazareth, who was crucified. He has risen; he is not here. See the place where they laid him." (Mark 16:6)

Mark records that "they went out and fled from the tomb, for trembling and astonishment had seized them, and they said nothing to anyone, for they were afraid" (Mark 16:8).

Again, it is difficult to be certain about the exact sequence of events, but this seems to be the most likely reconstruction. What is clear, beyond question, is that the tomb was empty and that the disciples came to faith through multiple encounters with the risen Lord.

The resurrection appearances

The disciples knew that the tomb was empty, and the angels had announced that Jesus had risen from the dead. But no one had yet seen the risen Lord.

Mary Magdalene returned to the empty tomb and wept. But her grief was turned to joy when Jesus appeared to her and called her by name. She went and told the disciples, "I have seen the Lord" (John 20:16, 18). This was the first resurrection appearance.

Meanwhile, the women who had remained at the tomb were so terrified by the appearance of the angel that they fled. But on the way, "Jesus met them" (Matthew 28:9). This was the second appearance of the risen Lord.

The Lord then appeared to Peter (Luke 24:34; 1 Corinthians 15:5), and to two disciples who were walking on the road to Emmaus (Luke 24:13–35). These were the third and fourth resurrection appearances.

The fifth appearance took place on the evening of that first Easter day, when the disciples were huddled together behind locked doors.

> Jesus himself stood among them, and said to them, "Peace to you!" But they were startled and frightened and thought they saw a spirit. And he said to them, "Why are you troubled, and why do doubts arise in your hearts? See my hands and my feet, that it is I myself. Touch me, and see. For a spirit does not have flesh and bones as you see that I have." And when he had said this, he showed them his hands and his feet. And while they still disbelieved for joy and were marveling, he said to them, "Have you anything here to eat?" They gave him a piece of broiled fish, and he took it and ate before them. (Luke 24:36–43)

Notice that the disciples' first reaction was to think that they were seeing a ghost. But then they heard Jesus speak. They touched

Him. They ate with Him. They saw His hands and feet. Jesus, who had been crucified, had risen from the dead.

The first word Jesus spoke to these frightened disciples was *peace*. All of them had forsaken Jesus when He was arrested in the garden of Gethsemane. They all knew they had failed their Master. But the risen Lord gave them *peace*.

Thomas was not present when the other disciples saw the Lord. He said to them, "Unless I see in his hands the mark of the nails … and place my hand into his side, I will never believe" (John 20:25).

Eight days later our Lord appeared for the sixth time. The disciples were together, and this time Thomas was with them.

> Although the doors were locked, Jesus came and stood among them and said, "Peace be with you." (John 20:26)

Thomas had said that he would not believe unless there was overwhelming evidence, and Jesus gave it to him: "Put your finger here, and see my hands; and put out your hand, and place it in my side" (John 20:27).

Jesus knew everything about Thomas, including his unbelief. But He still wanted Thomas to be His disciple. So, Jesus said to him, "Do not disbelieve, but believe" (John 20:27). What else was there for Thomas to do than to fall on his knees and confess, "My Lord and my God!" (John 20:28)?

Jesus did not write Thomas off because he refused to believe. He reached out to Thomas and led him to faith. Maybe you have struggled with faith. Perhaps you have felt that you could not believe. Jesus is ready to do the same for you.

So, how do we encounter the risen Lord? John answers that question directly.

> These are written so that you may believe that Jesus is the
> Christ, the Son of God, and that by believing you may have life in
> his name. (John 20:31)

Christian faith is not a blind leap in the dark. The compelling evidence on which we can take a reasoned step of faith in Jesus is placed before us in the Gospels. Thomas saw the hands and side of Jesus. We have not had that opportunity. But Jesus said, "Blessed are those who have not seen and yet have believed" (John 20:29).

The resurrection body

Jesus promised that all who believe in Him will share in His resurrection:

> "I am the resurrection and the life. Whoever believes in me,
> though he die, yet shall he live." (John 11:25)

All religions have some idea of life after death. But the resurrection is unique to Christianity. The good news is not simply that Jesus is alive, but that Jesus has risen! It is worth thinking about the difference.

The Son of God was alive in heaven before He took human

flesh. So why did He not simply leave His crucified body in the tomb and return to the Father? After all, it was only flesh and bone. Why bother with it?

The angels could still have appeared on Easter morning and said, "His body is here in the tomb, but don't worry, His spirit is with the Father in heaven." After all, isn't that precisely what we say at a funeral when a Christian dies?

But that's not what we find in the Gospels. Jesus said,

"For this is the will of my Father, that everyone who looks on the Son and believes in him should have eternal life, and I will raise him up on the last day." (John 6:40)

Human beings are a marvelous union of soul and body, and Jesus came into the world not to save a part of us, but to redeem the whole of us. He came to bring us, soul and body, into the joy of His presence forever.

QUESTIONS FOR REFLECTION AND DISCUSSION

 What is your first reaction to the empty tomb?

 Why do you think the disciples did not immediately assume that Jesus had risen from the dead when they discovered the empty tomb?

 Have you ever said, as Thomas did, "I will never believe"? If so, why?

 On a scale of 1 (weak) to 10 (compelling), what would you say about the evidence presented here for Jesus' resurrection? Why did you answer the way you did?

What difference would it make to your life if you truly believed that Jesus rose from the dead?

Born	Tempted	Crucified	Risen	**Ascended**
	30 years	3 years	3 days	40 days

After His resurrection, Jesus appeared to His disciples on multiple occasions in Jerusalem and Galilee. But Jesus had already told His disciples that He would return to the Father, and forty days after His resurrection, Jesus ascended into heaven (Acts 1:3, 9).

10

ASCENDED

AFTER THE FIRST resurrection appearances in Jerusalem, the disciples returned to their homes in Galilee. One night Peter went fishing with six of the other disciples. They spent the entire night in the boat but caught nothing. At dawn they saw a man on the shore who asked them, "Do you have any fish?"

"No," they answered.

He said to them, "Cast the net on the right side of the boat, and you will find some." So they cast it, and now they were not able to haul it in, because of the quantity of fish. That disciple whom Jesus loved [John] therefore said to Peter, "It is the Lord!" When Simon Peter heard that it was the Lord, he put on his outer garment, for he was stripped for work, and threw himself into the sea. The other disciples came in the boat, dragging the net full of fish. . . . Jesus said to them, "Come and have breakfast." (John 21:6–8, 12)

The purpose of the first resurrection appearances was clearly to bring the disciples to faith. Peter had seen the risen Lord on three occasions. James and John had seen him twice. Thomas had seen him once and confessed, "My Lord and my God!" So, by this time, the disciples knew that Jesus had risen from the dead.

Unbelief was a thing of the past for these men. So, if these disciples already believed that Jesus had risen, what was this appearance beside the lake about?

Peter, James, and John could not have missed the significance of this miracle. When Jesus first called them to follow Him, He told Peter to let down his nets for a catch. Peter had already toiled all night and caught nothing. But he obeyed the command of Jesus, and when he did, the nets were so full that two boats were barely able to bring them in. Then Jesus said to Peter, "Do not be afraid; from now on you will be catching men" (Luke 5:10).

Jesus had called His disciples to bring people to faith in Him, and in repeating the miraculous catch of fish, the risen Lord was re-affirming their calling.

Jesus has work for us to do

Sometime later, Jesus appeared to the disciples again on a mountain in Galilee. Matthew tells us that, "when they saw him they worshiped him, but some doubted" (Matthew 28:17). Believing in Jesus does not mean that you will never have any doubts. These men had seen the risen Lord, and some of them still had questions.

But Jesus did not wait for them to have perfect faith. He had work for them to do:

> "All authority in heaven and on earth has been given to me. Go therefore and make disciples of all nations, baptizing them in the name of the Father and of the Son and of the Holy Spirit, teaching them to observe all that I have commanded you." (Matthew 28:18–20)

Notice Jesus' three priorities: making disciples, baptizing them, and teaching them to live in accordance with His words and example. This commission is not only for the first disciples, but also for all of Jesus' disciples in every generation. As we pursue His commission, Jesus gives us this promise:

> "Behold, I am with you always, to the end of the age." (Matthew 28:20)

Jesus is in heaven

The last time Jesus appeared to His disciples was at the Mount of Olives in Jerusalem. His last words to them were about the work He had given them to do and the power He would give them to do it.

> "But you will receive power when the Holy Spirit has come upon you, and you will be my witnesses in Jerusalem and in all Judea and Samaria, and to the end of the earth." (Acts 1:8)

Then Luke records that

> when he had said these things, as they were looking on, he was lifted up, and a cloud took him out of their sight. (Acts 1:9)

Try to picture what the disciples saw: Jesus' feet left the ground and before their eyes, He *ascended*, ten feet, twenty feet, thirty feet, and then up into a cloud and beyond the range of their sight.

The ascension of Jesus was the work of God the Father, bringing Jesus back into heaven from where He had come. Jesus was "lifted up" (Acts 1:9). He was "taken up" (Acts 1:2); He was "carried up into heaven" (Luke 24:51). Jesus said, "I came from the Father and have come into the world, and now I am leaving the world and going to the Father" (John 16:28).

We might think that the disciples would be devastated by the departure of Jesus, but Luke tells us that that they "returned to Jerusalem with great joy" (Luke 24:52).

Why would the disciples have joy when Jesus left them?

Suppose you are in prison, charged with a serious crime. Your attorney is a man of great compassion, and when he visits your cell, you draw comfort from his presence. But you need more from your attorney than his comfort in the cell. You need him to represent you in the courtroom.

We need Jesus to represent us in heaven and, seated at the right hand of God the Father, Jesus is exactly where we need Him to be.

John says,

> My little children, I am writing these things to you so that you may not sin. But if anyone does sin, we have an advocate with the Father, Jesus Christ the righteous. (1 John 2:1)

When Jesus ascended, the disciples were filled with joy because they knew that in heaven, He would speak to the Father on their behalf. The book of Hebrews tells us that

> [Jesus] is able to save to the uttermost those who draw near to God through him, since he always lives to make intercession for them. (Hebrews 7:25)

Jesus intercedes for us, and what Jesus asks, the Father gives. Because He is in heaven, you will have all that you need for all that you face in every circumstance of your life.

Jesus will return

When Jesus ascended, an angel appeared to the disciples and said,

> "Men of Galilee, why do you stand looking into heaven? This Jesus, who was taken up from you into heaven, will come in the same way as you saw him go into heaven." (Acts 1:11)

Jesus is in heaven now, but He has promised that He will return: "I will come again and will take you to myself, that where I am you may be also" (John 14:3). When Jesus entered heaven, He opened heaven for us, and when He returns, He will take us home.

QUESTIONS FOR REFLECTION AND DISCUSSION

What is your first reaction to hearing that Jesus is in heaven, speaking to the Father on our behalf?

Do you have doubts about Jesus as some of the disciples did? Can you identify one right now?

Might one of the following be a next step for you?
1. Become a **disciple** and commit yourself to following Jesus?
2. Get **baptized** and publicly identify yourself as a follower of Jesus?
3. Join a church where you will hear the **teaching** of God's Word?

What circumstance in your life would you like to bring before God in prayer?

If Jesus were to return next week, would you feel ready to meet Him? Why or why not?

PART 3

FIVE GIFTS FOR EVERY BELIEVER

**The
Holy Spirit**   Faith   Forgiveness   The
                                        Church   Heaven

Jesus promised that He would always be with His disciples.
But since Jesus is in heaven, how can He be present with us on
earth? The answer is through the Holy Spirit. Jesus said,
"I will ask the Father, and he will give you another Helper,
to be with you forever, even the Spirit of truth" (John 14:16–17).
The "Spirit of truth" is the Holy Spirit, who is also referred to
as the Spirit of God, the Spirit of Christ, or the Spirit of Jesus.
The Holy Spirit is the Spirit of Jesus Himself, and what Jesus did
for His first disciples, the Holy Spirit does for all believers.

11

THE
HOLY SPIRIT

THE CHAIRMAN REPORTED that the church roll now stood at one hundred and twenty members. They did not own a building but were meeting in a room they had rented in the city.

The prayer meetings were well attended, and there had been a lot of discussion about how they should fill a vacant leadership position. But besides that, not a lot was happening.

The task of reaching their community was beyond these people. There were only a few of them, they had very little money, and outside of their meeting place, the culture had very little room for their message. That's what it was like for the church at the beginning of the book of Acts.

But Jesus had spoken about an event that would change all that.

In a few days, they would be "baptized with the Holy Spirit" (Acts 1:5).

They did not have to wait long. Just ten days after Jesus ascended into heaven, there was a festival called Pentecost. It was a big celebration, and Jerusalem was crammed with visitors from many countries (Acts 2:5). This was when the Holy Spirit was poured out on the church.

The gift of the Holy Spirit changes everything. The Holy Spirit convicts us of sin, brings us new life, generates faith in our hearts, and applies all that Jesus has accomplished for us on the cross so that we have peace with God, grow in likeness to Christ, and will finally be made perfect in heaven.

A sound like the wind

When the day of Pentecost arrived, they were all together in one place. And suddenly there came from heaven a sound like a mighty rushing wind, and it filled the entire house where they were sitting. (Acts 2:1–2)

In the ancient world, many languages use the same word for "wind," "breath," or "spirit." The sound of the wind is similar to the sound of breath, only it is much louder, and it lasts longer.

Before Jesus ascended into heaven, He breathed on His disciples and said, "Receive the Holy Spirit" (John 20:22). Jesus was explaining what would happen on the day of Pentecost.

So, when the disciples heard a sound like the rushing wind just a few days later, they would immediately associate it with the sound of Jesus breathing on them and recognize that this was the fulfillment of what Jesus had promised.

At the beginning of the Bible story, God breathed into Adam. A lifeless corpse lay on the ground until God gave it the kiss of life. Then Adam became a living being. The church is the body of Christ, but it was like a corpse until Jesus breathed the life of His Spirit into it. God breathed life into His people, and they were never the same again.

Great balls of fire

And divided tongues as of fire appeared to them and rested on each one of them. (Acts 2:3)

A ball of fire divided into individual flames, or "tongues" of fire, which came to rest on every person in the room. Something like this had happened before. In the Old Testament, God appeared to Moses in flames of fire resting on a bush. The amazing thing is that neither the bush nor the people were burned.

When God appeared in the fire, He commissioned Moses to lead His people out of slavery in Egypt. Now, on the day of Pentecost, God commissioned His church through the same sign.

Try to imagine yourself in the room as God's fire comes down. Who do you think it will land on? Peter? James? John? Or perhaps each of the twelve apostles?

As the fire comes down, it divides into separate flames. Looking up, you realize that one of these flames is coming toward you. And when you look around at the others in the room, you see that a flame rests on every one of them.

In the Old Testament, God gave His presence and power to *some* of His people. Now, He was giving His Spirit to *all* of them. God was commissioning every believer to advance His purpose in the world.

They spoke in other tongues

And they were all filled with the Holy Spirit and began to speak in other tongues as the Spirit gave them utterance. (Acts 2:4)

Suddenly and spontaneously, each of the hundred and twenty believers found that they were able to speak in languages they had never learned.

This was a reversal of what had happened long before. Early in the Bible story, God came down and broke the momentum of man's rebellion by confusing human language at the tower of Babel (Genesis 11).

It's not hard to imagine what happened. People who spoke the same language were drawn together. Then the different language groups separated from each other, spreading out across the face of the earth.

The Day of Pentecost was exactly the opposite. People from

every nation under heaven had gathered in Jerusalem (Acts 2:5), and when the Spirit of God came, they all heard the good news of Jesus Christ in their own language.

At Babel, the tongues were a judgment from God leading to confusion and people being scattered. At Pentecost, the tongues were a blessing from God leading to understanding and people being gathered.

To every tribe and nation

When the crowds in the city heard the sound of the wind, they headed in the direction from which it had come to see what was going on (Acts 2:6). When they arrived, they heard the believers declaring what God had done in different languages.

If you had been a visitor to Jerusalem that day, you would have looked for someone who spoke your language. And that's what happened. Small groups gathered round each of the believers, and they all heard what God had done in a language they could understand.

God's promise to bless all the families of the earth was being fulfilled, and it continues to be fulfilled today. The good news of what God has done in Jesus is for all people. God wants it proclaimed in every language. And all who believe have a part to play in communicating this good news.

Whose language can you speak? Perhaps you can speak in a way that children or young people can relate to. Maybe you can speak a language that will allow you to communicate with people from another culture. Maybe you can learn a language and be the means by which others hear the good news of Jesus.

God has put a circle of people around you, and you are the one who can bring the good news of what God has done to them.

Wind, fire, and tongues today

How should we understand the remarkable events on the day of Pentecost? God teaches us through the wind, the fire, and the tongues what He wants to do among His people.

God breathes life into His people. When that happens, the church is no longer an inward-looking organization that functions at a merely human level; it is a vibrant body filled with the life of God.

God commissions not just a few of His people for ministry, but all of us. The presence and the power of Almighty God rests upon every believer in the Lord Jesus Christ. And God's great purpose is that His blessing will flow to all nations through His people.

QUESTIONS FOR REFLECTION AND DISCUSSION

What is your first reaction to the gift of the Holy Spirit? Do you think you have received the gift of the Spirit? Why or why not?

How have you seen the Holy Spirit working in your life?

How have you seen the Holy Spirit working through others?

Who has God put around you that needs to hear about Jesus? How could you communicate the good news to them?

The Holy Spirit — **Faith** — **Forgiveness** — **The Church** — **Heaven** →

Faith is God's gift and His command. Jesus said, "Have faith in God" (Mark 11:22). That is a command. But faith is also God's gift. "For by grace you have been saved through faith. And this is not your own doing; it is the gift of God" (Ephesians 2:8). If you have felt that faith is beyond you, the good news is that Jesus is able to give what He commands.

12

FAITH

THE GOSPELS RECORD an occasion when Jesus got into a boat with His disciples and fell asleep. A storm came down on the lake and the boat began to fill with water.

The disciples woke Jesus and said, "Master, we are perishing!" (Luke 8:24). Jesus rebuked the wind and the waves, and there was a great calm. Then Jesus said to His disciples, "Where is your faith?" (v. 25). Jesus was not questioning the reality of their faith. He was questioning why they had not applied their faith to the situation they were in.

Faith must be applied. It does not work automatically. The heating system in your house works on a thermostat. You set the thermostat at the temperature you want to maintain, and when the temperature drops below that setting, your furnace comes on automatically.

But faith is not automatic. It involves an intentional engagement in which you trust Jesus in what you are facing right now.

Faith is like a muscle in the body that grows in strength as it is used. If you break your leg, your muscles will weaken because they are not being exercised. Muscles grow strong as they are stretched, and faith grows as it is applied in particular situations where you need to believe God's revealed promises and trust His hidden plans.

What faith is

Faith involves two elements. The first is believing in Jesus, the second is trusting Jesus, and these are two sides of the same coin.

Sometimes the word *believe* means knowing that something is true. James says that "even the demons believe—and shudder!" (James 2:19). The demons know that Jesus rose from the dead, and they tremble because of it, but faith is more than believing that certain things are true. Faith involves trusting the One we have come to believe.

We exercise faith by believing God in what He has revealed, and by trusting Him in what He has kept secret (Deuteronomy 29:29). God has revealed His Son and He has revealed His promises. But there are many things that God has kept secret. We do not know what tomorrow holds. But we trust God with what He has kept hidden, because we believe what He has revealed. God has said, "I will never leave you nor forsake you" (Hebrews 13:5). Faith says I can trust God for tomorrow because I believe the promise He has given today.

What faith does

Faith is like a living tree bursting with fruit.

1. Faith will open your understanding.

> By faith we understand that the universe was created by the word of God. (Hebrews 11:3)

2. Faith will lead you to work for the good of others.

> By faith Noah, being warned by God concerning events as yet unseen, in reverent fear constructed an ark for the saving of his household. (Hebrews 11:7)

3. Faith will lead you to obedience.

> By faith Abraham obeyed when he was called to go out to a place that he was to receive as an inheritance. And he went out, not knowing where he was going. (Hebrews 11:8)

4. Faith will give you hope.

> They desire a better country, that is, a heavenly one. (Hebrews 11:16)

5. Faith will bring blessing to others.

> By faith Isaac invoked future blessings on Jacob and Esau. (Hebrews 11:20)

6. Faith will lead you to worship.

> By faith Jacob, when dying, blessed each of the sons of Joseph, bowing in worship over the head of his staff. (Hebrews 11:21)

Why does faith do all these things? Where does its life and energy come from?

Faith unites us to Jesus

Faith unites us to Jesus Christ, so that we become His and He becomes ours. Jesus said,

> "I am the vine; you are the branches. Whoever abides in me and I in him, he it is that bears much fruit, for apart from me you can do nothing." (John 15:5)

The Bible describes a believer as a person who is *in Christ*.

> Therefore, if anyone is in Christ, he is a new creation. The old has passed away; behold, the new has come. (2 Corinthians 5:17)

It also tells us that Christ lives in us.

> I have been crucified with Christ. It is no longer I who live, but Christ who lives in me. And the life I now live in the flesh I live by faith in the Son of God, who loved me and gave himself for me. (Galatians 2:20)

Faith is the means by which we are joined to Jesus Christ so that His life flows in us.

The Bible uses the analogy of a marriage to describe this union.

> "Therefore a man shall leave his father and mother and hold fast to his wife, and the two shall become one flesh." This mystery is profound, and I am saying that it refers to Christ and the church. (Ephesians 5:31–32)

Marriage will change your life, and how it changes your life will depend on who you marry. Faith joins us to Jesus and makes us one with Him. For Jesus, this union meant being born in a stable, enduring temptation, and bearing our sins. For us, this union means receiving His unfailing love, His perfect righteousness, and His resurrection life.

If you are to enjoy this union, there must be a direct relationship between you and Jesus Christ, and this relationship has two conditions: One is that Jesus must receive you; the other is that you must receive Jesus.

In a wedding service, the groom is asked: "Will you take this woman to be your wife?" Then the bride is asked: "Will you take this man to be your husband?"

Two thousand years ago the question was asked of Jesus: "Are you willing to take on all that is involved in being united with sinners?"

And from the cross, with outstretched arms, Jesus answered: "I will."

Now, the Holy Spirit, who forges this union, asks you, *Will you take Jesus as your Savior and your Lord? Will you forsake all that displeases Him, and keep only to Him, as long as you shall live?*

And faith answers: *I will.*

As in the marriage service, the response "I will" could not be simpler. But these words of commitment are life-changing in their significance.

QUESTIONS FOR REFLECTION AND DISCUSSION

 What is your first reaction to the gift of faith?

What have you learned from the Bible that you have come to believe?

 Where do you most need to exercise faith in your life right now?

What is the difference between having faith in yourself and having faith in Jesus Christ?

Jesus made a commitment to us when He went to the cross. Have you committed yourself to Him?

The Holy Spirit   Faith   **Forgiveness**   The Church   Heaven

Jesus told a story about a son who left home, wasted his father's money and, in the end, became so desperate that he decided to return to his father. He expected a rather cold reception, but when he was still a long way off, his father saw him, came running to greet him, and welcomed him home with joy. This is a picture of how God receives us. When we come to Him in repentance and faith in Jesus, He embraces us with the wonderful gift of forgiveness.

13

FORGIVENESS

FORGIVENESS IS A BEAUTIFUL GIFT. When someone who has sinned repents and the one who was sinned against forgives, they are reconciled and both experience peace and joy.

The first step toward knowing this joy is to recognize how much we have been forgiven. Jesus teaches us that we should ask God to forgive our sins, which He describes as debts. "Forgive us our debts, as we also have forgiven our debtors" (Matthew 6:12; see also Luke 11:4).

We all have debts

Each of us lives in a network of relationships in which we have responsibilities and obligations. Only God stands outside of this network. God is no one's debtor, but we have an obligation to God and to others that can be summed up in a single word: love.

> "You shall love the Lord your God with all your heart and with all your soul and with all your strength and with all your mind, and your neighbor as yourself." (Luke 10:27)

When we think of our sins, we usually think first of wrong things we have done. But the starting point here is what we have failed to do. We owe God a life of devoted love every day, and what we owe, we have not paid.

We owe it to our neighbors to always seek their best interest. We owe a debt of love to our husbands, wives, parents, children, friends, coworkers, and even our enemies. And, however much we love, that debt is never fully paid.

We all have debtors

Debtors means that there will be people in your life who will not give you what they owe. We live in a fallen world, and just as you have defaulted on what you owe to God and to others, others will default on what they owe to God and to you.

God calls us to forgive those who have wronged us, failed us, and disappointed us, as He has forgiven us:

> Be kind to one another, tenderhearted, forgiving one another, as God in Christ forgave you. (Ephesians 4:32)

So the starting point for our forgiving others is the forgiveness we have received.

How can we be forgiven?

Jesus teaches us to pray, "Forgive us our debts" (Matthew 6:12). That is a big ask. Imagine going to someone to whom you owe $100,000 and saying, "I am asking you to write off this debt." But Jesus invites us to make a bigger ask of God.

When we ask God to forgive our sins, we come to Him with empty hands. We don't try to make a deal with God: "Father, I will make it up to You by being a good mother, a good student, or a good Christian." Instead, we say, "Father, I cannot pay. I ask You for mercy. Forgive my debt, wipe the slate clean, and cancel what I owe."

How can a just and holy God forgive our repeated failure to do what He commands? This question takes us to the heart of the Bible story. Jesus did what we have failed to do. He lived a life of perfect love. He fulfilled all that God requires of us, and then laid down His perfect life on our behalf. Jesus paid the debt we owe.

God forgives sinners as we look to His Son, Jesus, in faith and repentance.

> "Thus it is written, that the Christ should suffer and on the third day rise from the dead, and that repentance for the forgiveness of sins should be proclaimed in his name to all nations, beginning from Jerusalem." (Luke 24:46–47)

Suppose you came to God in repentance, and He said: "You are on probation and time will tell if your repentance is genuine." Now you must prove yourself, knowing that if you fail, God has it in for you. That would be an impossible burden.

But Jesus has something better for you than placing you on probation. When you come to Him in repentance, He pronounces you "Not guilty!" He forgives. He reconciles. And forgiveness is much better than probation!

> If we confess our sins, he is faithful and just to forgive us our
> sins and to cleanse us from all unrighteousness. (1 John 1:9)

> For as high as the heavens are above the earth,
>   so great is his steadfast love toward those who fear him;
> as far as the east is from the west,
>   so far does he remove our transgressions from us.
> (Psalm 103:11–12)

> There is therefore now no condemnation for those who are in
> Christ Jesus. (Romans 8:1)

Forgiveness is not God giving you an opportunity to prove yourself. Forgiveness is God dropping all charges against you and wiping your record clean forever.

How can we forgive?

Forgiveness is never easy. But if you are struggling to forgive another person, the good news is that receiving God's forgiveness will give you a new capacity to forgive others.

Jesus taught us to pray, "Forgive us our debts, as we also have forgiven our debtors" (Matthew 6:12). This means that there is the closest connection between us receiving forgiveness from God and us releasing forgiveness to others. The connection lies in the words *us* and *our*. The prayer is not "Forgive me my debts." It is "Forgive *us our* debts."

In praying this prayer, you are asking God to forgive not only the debts you owe but also the debts that others owe to you. "Father, forgive *us*" means, "Forgive me as I have failed to love You *and* forgive her as she has failed to love me." The only alternative would be: "Father, do *not* forgive us. I won't forgive, and I don't want You to forgive either." But who would want to pray that prayer? As God opens your heart to pour forgiveness out, it will be open for Him to pour forgiveness in.

QUESTIONS FOR REFLECTION AND DISCUSSION

What is your first reaction to the gift of forgiveness?

How would you describe the debt you owe to God?

On a scale of 1 (very little) to 10 (all of it), how much of your debt has been forgiven by God? Why?

Are you struggling to forgive someone right now?

How do you think God would respond if you came to Him in faith and repentance? Why?

**The
Holy Spirit**   **Faith**   **Forgiveness**   **The
Church**   **Heaven**

We have been looking at the gifts of the Holy Spirit, faith, and forgiveness. These are all wonderfully personal gifts: The Holy Spirit works in your life. When you have faith in the Lord Jesus Christ, He becomes yours. And when He is yours, forgiveness is yours. But there is more: when God reconciles you to Himself, He brings you into His family, and that brings us to the gift of the church.

14

THE CHURCH

WHAT COMES TO MIND when you think of the church? Stained glass windows? Hard wooden pews? Long dull sermons? The Bible says, "Christ loved the church and gave himself up for her" (Ephesians 5:25).

You can be sure that Jesus did not give Himself up for stained glass windows, wooden pews, and long dull sermons. So, what is the church and why did Jesus love her so much that He gave Himself up for her?

Jesus spoke of the church on just two occasions, and what He said defines what the church is for us.

What Jesus said about the church

The first time Jesus spoke about the church, He was referring to all believers in every time and place. Peter had confessed faith in Jesus, and Jesus said,

> "And I tell you, you are Peter, and on this rock I will build my
> church, and the gates of hell shall not prevail against it."
> (Matthew 16:18)

Jesus was speaking about all believers in every time and place:
"I will build *my church*"—singular! There is one church, comprising
all believers, and Jesus Christ builds it. And He has promised that
"the gates of hell shall not prevail" against this church.

Jesus was not referring to any local church or denomination.
All over the world there are sad stories of churches that have lost
their way and closed. But the church Jesus is building is alive and
well. It encompasses all believers in every time and place, and a large
part of it is already in heaven.

The second time Jesus spoke about the church, He was clearly
referring to a local gathering of believers.

> "If your brother sins against you, go and tell him his fault,
> between you and him alone.... But if he does not listen, take
> one or two others along with you.... If he refuses to listen to
> them, tell it to the church." (Matthew 18:15-17)

"Tell it to the church." This cannot possibly mean: "Tell it to all
believers in every time and place." No one could do that. Jesus was
clearly speaking here about a local congregation of believers.

So, our Lord used the word *church* in two ways: First, to describe
all believers in every time and place. Second, to describe a local

congregation of believers—called out by God to worship and sent out by God to serve.

The church is not a self-selecting group of people. It is never just you and a few of your friends. Jesus builds His church by bringing people to faith in Himself and gathering them in local congregations.

The purpose of God

How important is the church? If I have faith in Jesus, and have some good Christian friends, why do I need the church? The answer to these questions is: The church is central to God's purpose in the world. Paul speaks of

> the plan of the mystery hidden for ages in God, who created all things, so that through the church the manifold wisdom of God might now be made known to the rulers and authorities in the heavenly places. (Ephesians 3:9–10)

The rulers and authorities in the heavenly places are angels—spiritual beings created by God to worship and serve Him. God created all things so that His wisdom and His glory might be known. God will accomplish this "through the church."

When lost sinners are brought to Jesus, reconciled to God, and gathered together in His church, angels gasp and say, "Look at what God did!" When believers in local congregations love one another, despite our many differences, forgive one another for our many sins and failures, and put the needs of others before our own, angels see the beauty of God's grace displayed.

The church is central to the purpose of God, and being a member of Christ's church is a privilege we should cherish.

A glorious future

There is a big difference between what the church is now and what she will be. Look at any church today and you will find that it is a long way from what God calls the church to be. If this has been your experience, you may have given up on the church. But Jesus will never give up on His church.

> Christ loved the church and gave himself up for her, that he might sanctify her, having cleansed her by the washing of water with the word, so that he might present the church to himself in splendor, without spot or wrinkle or any such thing, that she might be holy and without blemish. (Ephesians 5:25–27)

Jesus *loves* the church with all her spots and wrinkles, and if we are like Him, we will love her too. Jesus *gave Himself* for the church, and if we are like Him, we will serve her too.

Notice what Jesus is doing for His church now. He cleanses her by washing her with His Word, the Bible. The Word of God is like a bath in which we are washed. This is the pattern of our life together. We are washed by the Word so that, gradually and increasingly, the beauty of Jesus may be seen in us.

Then we are told what Jesus will do for His church. He will

"present the church to himself in splendor, without spot or wrinkle ... that she might be holy and without blemish" (Ephesians 5:27). One day the church will be everything Christ calls her to be.

Think of the story of Cinderella. She is despised by her ugly sisters but destined to marry a prince. The church is despised by the world, but she is the bride of Christ, and her future is glorious. Jesus will present the church to Himself in splendor! And on that day, you will be so glad that you belong to His church.

QUESTIONS FOR REFLECTION AND DISCUSSION

What is your first reaction to the gift of the church?

Are you involved in a church? If so, how has it blessed you? What are some challenges you've faced?

If you are not involved in a church, what is keeping you away? Is there a nearby church you could visit?

What surprises you most about Jesus' plans for and commitment to the church?

What would you say to a person who is looking for the perfect church?

The Holy Spirit   **Faith**   **Forgiveness**   **The Church**   **Heaven**

The last gift God has prepared for us is the gift of heaven. Jesus said, "Father, I desire that they also, whom you have given me, may be with me where I am, to see my glory" (John 17:24). God's greatest gift is the gift of Himself. And one day, His people will be brought into the joy of His presence in heaven.

15

HEAVEN

THE LAST BOOK of the Bible tells us what God will do when human history comes to a close. God revealed this to the apostle John in a vision:

> Then I saw a new heaven and a new earth, for the first heaven and the first earth had passed away. (Revelation 21:1)

The joys of the new heaven and earth will be beyond anything we can imagine, but God uses two pictures to give us some inkling of what lies ahead for His people: The city and the garden.

> And I saw the holy city, new Jerusalem, coming down out of heaven from God, prepared as a bride adorned for her husband. (Revelation 21:2)

When John saw the new city coming down from heaven, he immediately recognized its skyline—Jerusalem! It was unmistakably familiar to him.

Jerusalem is full of significance in the Bible story. This was where God came down to meet with His people. The old Jerusalem *had* a holy place where the presence of God came down. The new Jerusalem *is* a holy place where God's presence will remain.

John heard a loud voice coming from the throne saying,

"Behold, the dwelling place of God is with man. He will dwell with them, and they will be his people, and God himself will be with them as their God. He will wipe away every tear from their eyes, and death shall be no more, neither shall there be mourning, nor crying, nor pain anymore, for the former things have passed away." (Revelation 21:3–4)

John saw the city from the outside and when, in his vision, he was invited inside the city, what he saw was a beautiful garden.

Then the angel showed me the river of the water of life, bright as crystal, flowing from the throne of God and of the Lamb through the middle of the street of the city; also, on either side of the river, the tree of life. (Revelation 22:1–2)

The Bible story began in a garden. There were trees in the garden and one of them was the tree of life. John would have seen the significance immediately—this is paradise restored, and the new paradise will be more glorious than the one Adam lost.

At the beginning of the Bible, God gave Adam and Eve the gifts of a home, work, marriage, and great joy in His presence. But, at the end of the story, God's people will have a better life, better work, better company, and greater joy than any of us have ever known.

Better life

Then the angel showed me the river of the water of life ... also, on either side of the river, the tree of life with its twelve kinds of fruit, yielding its fruit each month. (Revelation 22:1–2)

The garden of Eden was a wonderful home for Adam and Eve, but it never had trees that bore different kinds of fruit every month!

This is telling us that life in heaven will never be boring. There will always be something new. Jesus will always be leading us into fresh discoveries, and the greatest joys of your life in this world are just a small sample of the delights you will enjoy in God's new creation.

Better work

The throne of God and of the Lamb will be in it, and his servants will worship him ... the Lord God will be their light, and they will reign forever and ever. (Revelation 22:3, 5)

Notice what we will do in heaven: We will *worship*, we will *serve*, and we will *reign*. When God speaks about us reigning, He is telling us that life will be ordered and brought under our control.

We will no longer be subject to the tyranny of time. We will no longer be swept away by unpredictable tides of emotion or impulses of the will. We will no longer endure dysfunctional relationships.

And we will no longer be subject to danger or death.

Our lives will be ordered, our work will be fulfilling, and our relationships will be whole. We will serve God as we always wished we could, and all that we do will be offered to Him as worship.

Better company

The garden of Eden was enjoyed by just one man and one woman. But now a vast crowd is streaming in through the gates of God's city.

> It had a great, high wall, with twelve gates, and at the gates twelve angels . . . on the east three gates, on the north three gates, on the south three gates, and on the west three gates. (Revelation 21:12–13)

John saw twelve entrances to the new Jerusalem. The gates faced north, south, east, and west, and all of them were open (Revelation 21:25). At the beginning of the Bible story, the gate to paradise was closed. Cherubim guarded the entrance to the tree of life with a flaming sword.

But Jesus has broken the sword of judgment, and now angels are at the gates to welcome all who belong to Him. People are pouring in from every continent in the world—a vast company of people from every tribe and nation—all of them redeemed by Jesus Christ (Revelation 21:24–26).

Better joy

Our greatest joy in heaven will be the presence of God. God came down to the garden of Eden as a visitor and made Himself known, but in the new creation God will no longer be a visitor. God will dwell with His people, and we "will see his face" (Revelation 22:4).

God's ultimate gift is the joy of eternity in His presence, and He freely offers this gift to you: "To the thirsty I will give from the spring of the water of life without payment" (Revelation 21:6). Heaven is not a reward you can earn; it is a gift you must receive.

Jesus came into the world so that this gift could be yours. He went to the cross for you. He rose from the dead for you. He offers you everlasting life. But you must come.

> Let the one who is thirsty come; let the one who desires take the water of life without price. (Revelation 22:17)

Believe in the Lord Jesus Christ. Receive what He offers.

> The grace of the Lord Jesus be with all. Amen. (Revelation 22:21)

QUESTIONS FOR REFLECTION AND DISCUSSION

 What is your first reaction to the gift of heaven?

 What is one thing about heaven that catches your attention? What would you most enjoy?

 What promise from Revelation 21:3–4 is most encouraging to you? Why?

 How do you think you would respond to being in the presence of God in heaven?

 Are you confident that you will one day be in heaven? Why or why not?

ACKNOWLEDGMENTS

IT HAS BEEN MY JOY to work with friends, family, and colleagues on this project. Thanks are due first to Tim Augustyn. Presenting the Bible story through the lens of five people, five events, and five gifts was Tim's idea, and I am deeply grateful for all that he has contributed to this project. The many hours we spent pouring over this manuscript together have truly been a delight.

Sincere thanks to all of our Open the Bible team, and especially to John Aiello and John Martin, executive directors of Open the Bible in the US and the UK respectively. John Aiello leads and inspires us all with his relentless passion for putting the gospel within reach of every person. John Martin saw the potential of offering this material to churches and has contributed greatly to this project.

Working with the publishing team at Moody has again been a joy and delight. Randall Payleitner, Trillia Newbell, Kevin Mungons, and Richard Knox grasped the vision for this project and have given constant support and encouragement. Brittany Schrock did an outstanding job designing the covers. Thanks, Brittany for your patience and perseverance. We think it was well worth it. Thank you to all on the Moody team who have contributed to the publication of this book, and to Andrew Wolgemuth who guided this project from the beginning.

Special thanks also to my two eldest granddaughters, Jemma and Kylie (aged 11 and 10 respectively) who proofread the manuscript before it was sent to the team at Moody, and helped both by spotting some errors and by making some helpful suggestions. You both did a great job, and it truly was a joy for me to have you on the team!

And finally, a heartfelt thank you to my wife, Karen, for her love, patience, wisdom, support, and endless encouragement.

May the Lord use this short book for His glory and for the advance of the gospel,

Colin S. Smith